Qiu Xiaolong

—

Lines Around China

Qiu Xiaolong

Lines Around China

Neshui Publishing
St. Louis

Neshui Publishing
8029 Forsyth
Suite 204
St. Louis MO 63105
neshui.com

Cover design by Jay Babcock

ISBN 1-931190-99-2

CONTENTS

LINES OUT OF CHINA

Birds of Time	3
Cafe Talk	5
Justification	7
Birthday Night	8
Failure to See Yuanlu off	9
Gargoyle	10
Dover Peach	12
Winter Night	15
Poetry	16
Journey	17
The Sunlight Burning Gold	19
Illegal Immigrant Wife	20
Part and Parcel of Poetry	22
Answer to a Friend's Question	24
Time Difference	25
That's Me	27
An Orientalist Recipe	29
To Xiangxiang	30
Connections	32
Not Meeting Someone in London	33
Meeting Someone in Paris	34
To My Wife	35

LINES IN CHINA

Ragged Shoes of the Cultural Revolution	39
Parting	41
Love Story	42
When Nixon First Visited China	43
On the Back of a Photograph	46
For Rosenthal, a Poet	47
The White Dream	48
Don Quixote	49

Fish Tale   51
Lost   53
Theme   54
To a Friend Who Reads Lacan   55
Pill and Picture   56
Other's Interpretation   58
Snowman   59
Fragment   60
To C   61

CATHAY REVISITED

About Wang Changling   65
Apologies to Zhangji   66
Men Haoran's Spring Morning   67
Drink to Li Bai   68
Thinking of Li Shangyin at Yaddo   69
Reading Li Shangyin at Night   71
Fantasies about Xue Tao   72
After Su Shi   73
Liu Yong's Relevance   75
Translation of Ma Zhiyuan   77
Comparative Poetics   78

ACKNOWLEDGEMENT

In this collection I have included some of the poems written in the last four years, a period in which I have been busy working on novels and translations, and have made frequent trips to China. This is why the collection is divided into three parts. The poems of the first section, *Lines out of China*, were written in the US. *Lines in China* are poems written during my trips there, as well as some translations of poems I had written years earlier in Chinese. *Cathay Revisited* is a result of my dialogue with classical Chinese poets in the translation of their works.

I want to thank my friends Mona Van Duyn, Jarvis Thurston, Carol Wantz and Susan Lagunoff, who have not forgotten to ask about my poems when reading my novels and translations. I especially want to thank Michael Castro, who carefully read the manuscript and gave me valuable suggestions. But for their wonderful support, this volume would exist only as unfinished computer files.

In October, during a book tour in San Francisco, Caroline Cummins interviewed me about my novel *A Loyal Character Dancer*, and then I read a not-too-surprising statement in the review published afterward: "Poetry is his proxy."

She may be right. I hope so.

Some of the poems here have appeared in my novels, as well as in magazines, though they have been modified slightly since then.

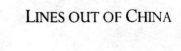

LINES OUT OF CHINA

BIRDS OF TIME

Afterwards, your hair
still wet from shower, shopping
at the Shanghai First Department Store,
you wound yourself up in a plush duckling
waddling on the counter, squawking,
"After each time, you buy me a fluffy darling—
In one year, we'll have a room
full of swaggering sillies."
It's silly, but so were many other things,
we contemplated – the long line standing
for American visas, curving
overnight into a huge question mark,
an old waiter's shock at us sharing
a tiny bowl of noodles, or Eliot saying
April is the cruelest month.
It's April, hyacinth blossoming
out of your bare arms
into the heart of the neon light
ceaselessly changing, as the world
in our interpretation.
Then—

Separation
surprising reunion, and unsurprising
separation, in another country.
Time flies, before your voice
finally flutters back, still familiar,
yet laden with the travel fatigue
of an investment banker
in an unexpected international call,
"Now I make a deposit wherever
I cut a deal, Toronto, Hong Kong, Melbourne,
or Tokyo. We've bought a Porsche
and a Bostonian condo overlooking a lake
where swans come and go.
In Shanghai today. Still remember—
two literature students, years ago, too poor
to afford a roast Beijing duck
in a shabby restaurant?"

At night, the dry creek
under my bay window appears
skeleton white in the moon,
no bird there.

CAFE TALK

Creamy coffee, cold;
toy bricks of sugar cubes
crumbling, a butter blossom still
reminiscent of natural freedom
on the mutilated cake,
the knife aside, like
a footnote. It is said
some people can tell the time
by the change of color
in a cat's eyes—
but you can't.
Doubt, a heap of ancient dregs
from the bottle of *GREAT WALL*,
rests in the sparkling wine.

Under the play of neon lights
the Uygur girl on the wall
is carrying grapes to you:
infinite motion, light
as a summer in grateful tears
when a bit of the golden paint,
under her bangled bare feet,
flakes from the frame around her.

5

Nothing appears more accidental
than the world in words.
A rubric turns by chance
in your hands, and the result,
like any result, is called history.

Through the window we see no star.
Mind's square deserted, not a pennant
left. Only a rag picker of the ages
passes by, dropping scraps
of every minute into her basket.

JUSTIFICATION

A withered tree turns out to be
ideal for the termites, which
legitimate the noise of
a philosopher-billed woodpecker
in the woods, where a henpecked hunter
skulks in dread of his wife,
half-heartedly raising his gun.

Once, a girl lectured me
on politics and logic, her
bare shoulder rippling
under my palm: "Do whatever
you want; you'll always find reasons
later." An apple rolled
out of her picnic hamper. Snatches
of a *pipa* melody drifted
from a blue boat. I lost myself
in her cascading hair, which
smelled of barbecued ribs.

BIRTHDAY NIGHT

3:30 A.M. A dog barks
against the moon-bleached night.

Is the dog barking into my dream
or am I dreaming of the dog?

FAILURE TO SEE YUANLU OFF

How long ago was Li Bai moved
by his friend's song
on parting at Peach Blossom Lake—
one early autumn morning,
a lone sampan sailing
into the ceaselessly warring clouds
of the mid-Tang dynasty?

The wind that breaks a petal
breaks me.

By the Missouri River,
April's cruelest fingers are fastening
onto a hook a bait of cricket—
or a bait of me?
Oh, the pierced brown wings
that start scratching a muffled note.

At the moment of leaving,
your lectures on Oriental poetry
still undelivered, do you hear it,
Yuanlu, my singing in another language,
hollow as the broken wings
screeching toward Lambert Airport?

GARGOYLE

It was on a hillside, Jingshan Park, Forbidden City,
where the Qing Emperors had succeeded
the Ming Emperors, we sat
on a slab of rock there, watching
the evening spread out against the tilted eaves
of the ancient, splendid palace.
Below us, waves of buses flowed
along the Huangchen Road—a moat,
hundreds of years ago. We murmured
words in Chinese, then in English
we were learning. The bronze stork,
which had once escorted the Qing Dowager
stared at us. You dreamed of us becoming
two gargoyles, you told me,
at *Yangxing* imperial hall, gurgling
all night long, in a language comprehensible
only to ourselves. A mist
enveloped the hill. We saw a tree
hung with a white board saying
"It's on this tree that Emperor Chongzhen
committed suicide," reminding me
of the blackboard hung round my father's neck
during the Cultural Revolution. The evening

struck me as too cold. We left the park.
Later, I left the country.

Tonight, sleepless
in St. Louis, fired from a bagel shop
for my Chinese accent, I think
of you again—still gurgling,
gurgling on the hillside of Jingshan,
through the night, in a language
all of your own?

The shop neon sign says:
Gargoyle.

DOVER PEACH[*]

Here I am, standing with the girl
who once stood with Matthew Arnold
on the Dover beach, then
with Anthony Hecht too, now we find
ourselves in the penthouse
of the Shanghai Hotel, overlooking
the Bund stretching along the Huangpu River
in the ebb and flow of neon lights
like the folds of a bright girdle
unfurled. She's pretty, you
know, with all her professional makeup,
almost perfect on the television:
CEO, Dover Peach Cosmetics Incorporation,
marketing her new product to China.
Too busy, she's forgotten all about Sophocles,
but not the origin of her brand name.

"Poor old Matthew, he clutched me
like his last straw, moaning
with the melancholy, long, withdrawing roar
of passion, and then weeping

---

[*] The present poem is inspired by two related poems, Matthew
Arnold's "Dover Beach," and Anthony Hecht's "Dover Bitch," though
it is not exactly meant as a parody.

12

about the helpless receding Sea of Faith,
though like everybody else, he got such a lot
out of me. Royalties, critics' raving, not
to mention the ravishing time
with my undulating body— *the waves...*
begin, and cease, and then again
begin. Anthony's much worse, thinking
how to capitalize Matthew
through me, his dirty whiskers
tickling my bare back, *moon-blanched,*
with tremulous cadence slow
and fast, and he got those lines anthologized,
and his tenure secured. Did he bring me
a bottle of Nuit d'Amor? No. I took him
out of pity. Not you, President Joe,
of East-West, you know how to ripen me
into a real Dover Peach,
juicy, palatable, bursting to your touch.
Oh, you don't have to be jealous.
I'm telling you the stories
about those poor, pathetic men of letters
as you can make the best use of it
in our marketing campaign."

In the soft light, her small toe,

dainty, snowy, as creamy as a scallop
in the hotel chef's midnight special.
I'm starving again.

Afterwards,
in lingering ecstasy, I forget myself
and murmur about *"ignorant armies clash
by night,"* a fragment I analyzed years ago
in my unfinished dissertation,
a business secret I have kept from her.

WINTER NIGHT

Crossing Skinker at night,
I feel the leaves fall in the starlight,
and my frozen thoughts, too,
to the foreign ground.

The moon shines as bright,
perhaps, as on your TV
in Shanghai, the tenderness
of a tealeaf between your lips.

Back home at 8:30
with five or six small fish in the plastic pail,
including a baby bluegill
which could hardly count,
a water snake, its triangular head smashed
into a rotten persimmon—still, not
too bad a day, I have to say, a sunburned nose
peeling under the scrutiny of my wife
who, discovering a China-like map
of mosquito bites on my bare back, snaps:

What's the point—nine hours
under the scorching sun, you have
to buy the gasoline, the drink, the bait,
two hot dogs, half a pack of Camels, and
now these tiny fish, three bucks' worth
in a market, you are really hooked.

An accountant, she sees no point
calculating a split-second
of catching the golden sun
in silver scales.

JOURNEY

You keep on murmuring the name
of each new platform
each time the train slows
down, as if anxious to make sure
you are not losing yourself
to an unchanging aisle with changing feet,
in black loafers, in shiny boots, in red slippers,
in muddy sandals, coming and going.

Destination is not
on the unfolded map, nor
in the punched tickets. Here is
never where you want to be.

Snow falls in the evening.
You turn to a light shimmering
on the window and a fly circling
its upper corner. Every time
you raise your hand, it drones away—
only to return buzzing
around the same spot, inexplicably, like a cliché.

Overnight, the land is buried
in white. Breathing hard
against the pane, you try to wipe
the vapor away with your hand, when
you see the window frame your ever returning
reflection—like a fly.

THE SUNLIGHT BURNING GOLD

The sunlight burning gold,
we cannot collect the day
from the ancient garden
into an album of old.
Let's pick our play,
or time will not pardon.

When all is told,
we cannot tell
the question from the answer.
Which is to hold
us under a spell,
the dance or the dancer?

Sad it's no longer sad,
the heart hardened anew,
not expecting pardon,
but grateful, and glad
to have been with you,
the sunlight lost on the garden.

ILLEGAL IMMIGRANT WIFE

(From a Roach's Perspective)

Afterwards, you rise
to massacre us in the kitchen,
seeking us above the spill
of moldering bowls and pots, chasing us
among the bottles of soy sauce,
oyster oil, and fermented bean curd,
driving us out of the Thai rice bag,
and then kneeling by the sink,
as if in prayer, you start
an intensified search over the floor
scattered with our bodies, your thighs and legs
dazzling through your nylon robe
unbelted, still reeking of sex.
The scarlet jasmine-embroidered slipper
in your hand jumps the chopsticks
into crosses, and you jump to grind us
under your soft, round toes.
Your hair flashing against the dreary wall
turns the night into a delirium
of human refugees fleeing
from a faraway land.
O God!

The light off
we see a man taking
you from behind, savagely,
like one of us.

PART AND PARCEL OF POETRY

The gray swivel chair belonged to Takahashi,
a Japanese girl born in Hiroshima,
who studied Deconstruction on a Persian rug
in her St. Louis apartment, sitting
in her kimono, her red-painted toenails like petals
blossoming out of *The Tale of Genji*—
the topic of her dissertation. She gave
the chair to me before she went back
for her research in Tokyo, where she discovered
she had lung cancer, and passed away
with her dissertation unfinished.

"Take this long desk, your daughter
may use it one day for a ping pong table,"
Don smiled through the fading evening light, tapping
on the wooden top, like an ancient palace door.
A glaring leftover of his moving sale,
customer-designed, the desk was long enough
to spread a dozen books in a row. A poetry
professor all his life, Don found a line break
the only break he needed, working
at the desk, his skies full of soaring butterflies
of prizes, when his publisher went
bankrupt one month before his retirement.

22

A blue balloon popped amid children's laughter.

This antique Huizhou writing brush
of scarlet skunk tail came
from Yuanlu. A visiting scholar
of the classical Chinese, too obsessed
with the image of the brush tip
softened on a girl's tongue
in Li Shangyin's lines to pound
on the unfeeling computer keyboard,
he went back to China, asking me
to keep the touch
of a Tang brush— "for inspiration."

I have not been thinking of them
all the time in the busy world
of words, but they are part and parcel
of my poetry; sometimes, the chair,
now totally frayed, creaks in a way
reminiscent of Lady Purple's somnambular night
in *The Tale of Genji*; the desk still solid,
works out occasional mosaics of fragments
inconceivable on a PC monitor; and once
or twice, I pick up the antique pen
absentmindedly, turning myself
into a soft writing brush tip.

23

ANSWER TO A FRIEND'S QUESTION

Why fish?

          A wish
to feel the reel
casting an arch across the blue skies
with a sense of clutching fate
in the hand, though still
subject to luck's swish—

              like fish.

TIME DIFFERENCE

It's growing light at six
in the morning. Looking out
toward Delmar, I see an old couple
standing in their flowing robes,
by the newsstand, unfolding
the newspaper, pointing, talking, and patting
each other's shoulder, so meaningful
to themselves—none of their words
audible across the distance—
like a shadow play
on a Beijing temple fair stage.

Seven o'clock in the evening
in Beijing. What are you doing
at this moment? As years ago,
I recall, biking back through a maze
of winding lanes, carrying my books
on your rack, gliding by the white and black
sihe style houses, a peddler selling orange
paper wheels, old people practicing
tai chi, a pigeon's whistle tailing
high in the clear sky, your bike bell spilling
into the tranquil air…you

coming back the moment when
the *Beijing Evening Post's* about
to unfold me, and you must fold me
in your arms, in spite
of all the meaningless news.

THAT'S ME

(Picture in a Poetry Anthology)

Carol wanted me to wear
my black Polo Club suit and
to have a gray Mao jacket
displayed in her studio background—
a footnote to the cultural conflict
in my work. A super idea,
I agreed, and spent the long afternoon posing
with the Mao jacket stretched out
through a clothesline, taped on the wall
like a postmodernist painting, or spread out
on the floor, almost a perfect peddler's setting...
After three Kodak rolls, she declared
her job done and treated me
to beer and peanuts; I demonstrated
to her the technique of picking up a peanut
with bamboo chopsticks.
She took a picture of it, giggling.

The anthology came out, finally, to show
me holding a Bud Light
in one hand, chopsticking
a peanut in another, smiling

in a black suit—
an unmistakable image of a salesman
That's me, selling the Oriental,
with the Occidental.

        You may also see,
(with the right perspective) the shadow,
my right elbow presents on the wall,
a silhouette of a crane musing
with a long, exotic bill of chopsticks
as in a classic Chinese scroll.
The Mao jacket disappeared,
out of focus, perhaps.

AN ORIENTALIST RECIPE

(Reading Richard Jones's "Wanchu's Wife in Bed")

Some indispensable ingredients:
Her thighs, marinated for an hour
in oyster sauce, yellow rice wine, chopped ginger,
MSG, egg white, brown sugar, and *taibai* cornstarch;
her small bound feet (Ming dynasty style) cut
sharp-pointed as if to scissor the night
into slices of imagination, and his black queue
(Qing dynasty style) coiling her breasts
like a snake; stir-fry over high heat; throw in a ladle
of Maotai when *Yin* and *Yang* merge
into each other in the wok; add XO sauce
on her tender loins writhing under Wan Chu, moaning,
murmuring about Wang Chen instead (Who is
Wan Chu, or Wang Chen, does not matter.
To sound Oriental is all). For special flavor,
put a string of red peppers like lanterns
illuminating reflections on the rice paper windows,
and spread a handful of chopped green scallion
around her belly, amorously
aromatic. The best time to serve:
sizzling hot, melting on your tongue.

XIANGXIANG

It's not the river, but the moment
the river came flowing into your eyes...
We stood at Huangpu Bridge, overlooking
a sampan tied to a stump, swaying
under our gaze. A wave, and a cloth diapers
fell from a clothesline stretched across the deck.
"All the possibilities of the world
bobbing in a sampan cabin," I said. "A torn sail
married to an broken oar," you said,
a bubble of metaphor rising
from your tongue tip, iridescent
in the sun. A naked baby appeared
crawling out of the tarpaulin mat, as if
born of our expectation. Reaching
into your satchel, you produced the last apple
to an infant smile. Two literature students,
we had little, but thought we had the world
in the words.

At Riddle's Bar
on Delmar, marketing magnesium
for the maximum profit margin
over Bloody Mary, I feel the hard rock

rolling the room like a sampan swaying
in the river, a wind-blown napkin reminding me
of a letter to you returned as "undeliverable"
as the room is suddenly blacked out—
The light back, a blonde singer stalks
over to the table, high in her heels, chewing
gum, blowing out a bubble
as beautiful as yours.

Wind blows us out, a bubble going
like a dream, then gone.

CONNECTIONS

Sitting on the front steps
of the Kingsbury Animal Hospital
closed at night, my car broken down,
chewing a cold chicken leg, no dogs
or cats around, a pile of Feng Shui books
from Olin library, watching the leaves
of curious eyes blinking under the stars,
cars flowing like a childish river.

There is nothing more incongruous
than thinking about it

I can be connected to anything,
or anything, to me.

32

NOT MEETING SOMEONE IN LONDON

It is not we who sing the song,
but the song that sings us—
Better not to meet now
than to meet...

So we bury our heads
into the desert of memories.

Look, an ostrich plume (yours,
or mine?) trembling
on a hat of the last century
in somber Kensington Palace.

Leaves and leaves outside are whispering
in green conversation.

MEETING SOMEONE IN PARIS

Holding two cups of black coffee
in St Germain, we try to stir
our memories with the coffee spoons
as in a poem we read together, long ago,
on a green bench in Bund Park,
with a petrel flying out of the morning mist
that was already fading, then
and there, with the sugar cube
of the present moment crumbling
like the debris of imagination.

The logo of the scarlet Guess appears
blurred on your bosom—
as on that first page you accidentally
dropped a red ink stain
which, once, we compared
to a maple leaf against the snow...

To My Wife

You are wearing yourself out
against me. A piece
of sandpaper. Shining,
I shun the rust between your lips.

LINES IN CHINA

RAGGED SHOES OF THE CULTURAL REVOLUTION

The Cultural Revolution hung
a halter of ragged shoes
around her neck: heels,
mules, slings, boots, sandals,
her bare feet bleeding...

"Why those ragged shoes?" a boy asked his grandfather in the midst of the spectators that lined the street like spring bamboo shoots after a rain. "Symbolic," his grandfather said. "Heaven alone knows how many men might have had her." "Like those dirty shoes," his father said, "she must have been worn out by such a number of them. What a notorious actress before 1949!" "But that was almost thirty years ago," the boy said "Thirty years ago," his uncle cut in, "you could not have touched her little toes with thousands of Yuan. Today, I have placed a wreath of shoes on her neck." "So those are your own shoes," the boy nodded in enlightenment, staring at people's spittle shining on her face, and a red line of footnotes drying behind her.

Her mad song to the ragged shoes:

Shoes, shoes, shoes, shoes
of the Cultural Revolution;
shoo, shoo, shoo, shoo,
barefoot is the solution.

PARTING

Missing the midnight bus that passed
by your window, I walked back,
amidst the leaves falling like the bamboo slips
for divination in an ancient temple, darkly
portentous. Moving
through Heaven Food Market, I saw
a long line of baskets—
plastic, bamboo, rattan, wood, straw—
of all shapes and sizes, stretching
up to a counter with a sign of *yellow croaker*,
a fish so popular in Shanghai, the baskets
left standing for the virtuous wives who would soon come,
picking their positions in the line, eyes dreamy
with their husbands' satisfaction...Bang,
bang, bang, a night worker
cracked a gigantic frozen bar of the fish,
blow after blow, faceless in an upturned collar
of his cotton-padded overcoat.

How we really parted, I forgot.

LOVE STORY

Afterwards,
it is a book he opens and closes anytime,
anywhere, as he pleases,
the cover half torn, one page dog-eared
another jelly-smeared, most of them underlined
or highlighted, hardly intelligible to himself
next morning, and crossed out, black and blue
all over, in short:
his book—
    which tells a story about him.

WHEN NIXON FIRST VISITED CHINA

Commissar Liu, the red-armbanded
commander of the *"Neighborhood Patrol,"*
had not yet come in. Not
a mouse stirring, the lane held
its breath as if awaiting
resurrection—in accordance

to the Party authorities' instruction:
*"China should show the proletarian best
to the first American president."*
Commissar Liu had demanded invisibility
of washing lines, beggars, wok smoke,
and put all of us, nose running kids,

in Granny Wang's attic. Curiosity crazed
caged cats. Lihua studied the contour
of Rocky Mountains in the rain-stained
ceiling; Xiaoying, hiding-&-seeking
among a sweep of drying pantyhose,
developed a dacron-allergy (years

later, dumped due to her incessant sneezing);
I turned into a paper airplane only
to be immediately caught and shot
in an "espionage mission" to see
what was not supposed
to be seen in the newspapers.

Granny started hugging a clay Buddha image:
Come Commissar, allow us to cook,
and to cough. Then, far away,
Commissar Liu finally caught a glimpse
of the waitress in *Yellow Dragon Bar*
at the City God's Temple Market,

where, earlier in the afternoon,
President Nixon had described her as
"cute," smacking his lips. A queue
instantly formed outside the window, looking
through the glass, at her cutting
a Beijing roast duck, its fat dripping

from the stitched ass. An iridescent-eyed
fly sucked the duck sauce
on her bare toes. A fire hydrant
stared in outrage. The red armband crumpled

in his pocket, he forgot us.

    We did not
know the political incident until years
later, when Comrade Liu (having lost
his Commissarship because of it)
married the waitress, no longer
a "City Goddess" after Watergate,
and I started learning English.

ON THE BACK OF A PHOTOGRAPH

Passing, passing, passing
the waves behind you, the petrel
behind you, even the horizon
against the darkening
sky behind you.
A statue
against time, at least
in the photo, you feel
the spray catching, caressing
your bare legs and feet
with ancient sighs.

FOR ROSENTHAL, A POET

Whatever it is, it must have
the monomania of a mule
to circle, blindfolded,
the mill, dragging all the weight
its back can endure.

Whatever comes out of the mill
will not go to its muzzled mouth:
the world, when seen
without the black cloth,
is a muddled mishap.

THE WHITE DREAM

Again, the white dream
is leaping heartily
among the ocean of weeds
as you slowly raise your gun.

Distantly, the smoke darkening
the corner of the skies,
you remain standing
motionless with the knowledge
that awaiting you
is either the bloody reality
or nothing. The setting sun
gilds a statue coldly.

DON QUIXOTE

Once more, you are going to mount that bony horse,

old, tired, dispirited, like your beaten self

A cloud of dust rises on the road,

nothing but dust,

and you uphold your shield, as if

it were the setting sun of an ancient empire.

In a bronze reflection

you discover a broken figure, identifiable

only in the shape of a rusty suit

of armor that keeps you going, too busy

going to recognize yourself.

Recognizable or not,

what choice do you have?

A role played too long, inevitably,

plays you. You dare not lie

under the ash tree, or doubts,

like termites, will hollow your trunk.

What shines, you shield your eyes

with the back of your hand, shines

in your mind only.

       Dear Sancho,

dumb, dutiful as ever, shoulders

a newly fixed lance, looking

up at you, waiting.

He, too, has to find himself

something to do, dragging his feet

along the unfamiliar road,

wondering.

FISH TALE

Here we are, *big bucks* in a dry month, sweating,
swearing, and studying the menu
at a sampan-shaped saloon.
in the Forbidden City. A young waitress
recommends to us the chef's special,
"Qianlong's live carp so tender
its eyes still turning
on a willow-pattern platter—"

Emperor Qianlong, of the Qing dynasty, traveled
in the disguise of a merchant, boarded
a sampan on a stormy night,
wet, cold, hungry
as a wolf. A fishing girl, alone in the boat,
fried a carp she had just caught,
which proved too large
for the wok, with its head and tail sticking
out of the sizzling oil. Cooked,
served under the awning
of the tung-oiled boat,
the fish tasted extraordinarily tender,
its eyes goggling once or twice in the dark—
Or something he imagined

in his cup? The fish appeared
as if turning into the girl, bleeding
and thrashing, and he fell to sucking
her small toe like a dainty ball
of the live carp cheek meat.

"A chef's special with a legend,"
the waitress finishes her introduction
with the menu in the hand, turning
into the fishing girl, her feet bare,
silver-bangled, lighting
the red carpet, as we fall
on the savory meat.

LOST

That morning, I awoke
to a Qing dynasty scroll hanging
over the spill of your hair—
high above, the mountains lost in the clouds,
and the clouds lost, too, in the mountains,
at the bottom, leaning upon a bamboo stick,
an old man looking up, lost
in contemplation of the mountains and clouds

"You have to lose yourself," I
said, "before you may hope to be
part of a picture."

"A new self
in the loss of selves," she
said, "like last night?"

THEME

Finally, when he decides to knock
at the door, it opens
into an empty room, where
he finds only himself,
snow-covered, staring out
of an ancient bronze mirror.

Silence anchored
by a blue velvet slipper
under the marble coffee table,
the other one missing, several pits,
smeared with ash and mildew, still
reminiscent of her luscious cherry lips
in a shell-shaped ashtray.

A white crane stalks
through the window-framed night
its footsteps appearing
and disappearing in the snow.

It is morning again.
The wall presents the familiar frown
of the flying Apsaras.
A fly makes up her belly button.

TO A FRIEND WHO READS LACAN

The bookmark puts you among the pages
where you wish to forget.

Everything is imaginable, but not innocent.
Looking out the window, you see
a *tung*-oiled paper umbrella
unfolded on the porch,
red-pointed,
as a gigantic breast, swaying in the wind.

You take the chair as the sight
of the shapely arms takes your mind.

In the valley, the echo brings
itself to face what it is not.

PILL AND PICTURE

In the summer of 1972, he suffered
a nervous breakdown after a long afternoon
of discussing a poem in praise
of Chairman Mao, of stirring black coffee
with "political correctness," and he was seized
with an impulse to blaspheme
the sacred lines. Sweating, stuffing a fist
into his mouth, as if battling toothache,
he scurried home, skunk-like, to a handful
of sedatives, to awake, next morning,
a scared scarecrow.
What if the compulsion overwhelmed him again?
The week before, a counter-revolutionary
executed for the crime of carrying
a Mao's statue on his back
 (for convenience's sake) with a rope tied
around the plaster neck. He decided
to carry in his wallet a packet
of sedatives, hiding them
behind the picture of a girl wearing
a gold badge of Mao. Natural,
perhaps, for him to touch the picture
time and again—to make sure

of the tranquilizer being there, available
through her gaze.

        He recovered
in 1976, after the Cultural Revolution,
the picture yellowed with time,
with the chemical reaction behind.
(Had the pills tranquilized the passion?)
Having broken up with her, he had the wallet
lifted one cold winter day—to the pickpocket,
the pills, long pulverized, might have looked
like some drying material, he thought,
that protected a precious picture.

OTHERS' INTERPRETATION

Where do we live?
In others' interpretation,
where we find ourselves framed,
posing against a walnut tree whispering
in the wind, or a butterfly soaring
into the black eye of the sun

So you and I, too, have
to keep ourselves in the proper light,
and the proper position too,
to be recognized as meaningful, as
a woodpecker must prove its existential value
in the echoes of a dead trunk.

Still I am holding out to you
a bouquet of words
that may blossom fleetingly
in your smile, then fade.

SNOWMAN

You have to be a snowman
to stand in the snow,
listening to the same message
of the howling wind
with imperturbable patience,
gazing at the scene
without losing yourself in it,
while a hungry, homeless crow
starts to peck your red nose,
apparently, a carrot

FRAGMENTS

The beach stretches forward
with your footprints...

Spray disappears
among your bare toes,
and appears
in another's dream.

To C

In the beginning, it is a grain
of sad sand wearing and tearing
your heart, a secret
that keeps your eyes
secreting day and night
in endless revolving, revolving
revolving around the silent, splendid sun,
a sore that keeps growing
until you are nothing but containment
of the sore—a suffering so enormous
that it turns your life
to a worthless shell.

                To a shell
what's the value
of a pearl, however precious?

CATHAY REVISITED

ABOUT WANG CHANGLING*

The chilly rain falling all night
in the Wu River...
At dawn, you had to see off your guest
against the Wu mountains
which, of a sudden, appeared so solitary.
"If my folks and friends ask about me
in Luoyang, tell them:
An ice-pure heart, a crystal vase."

I am the one who left you there
over a thousand years ago,
traveling across mountains and rivers,
still repeating your message
in another language.

---

* Wang Changling, (?-756?) a well-known Tang dynasty poet.

APOLOGIES TO ZHANG JI*

The moon setting, the crow cawing,
the frost spreading out against the sky,
the maple trees, the fisherman's light moving
across the river, who's there,
worried even in sleep?
By the Cold Mountain Temple
out of Gusu City,
a sampan approaches in the midnight bells.

I come on a summer day,
along a road full of construction noise,
to catch a glimpse
of the celebrated Tang dynasty poem
carved on an ancient stone tablet,
and to take a picture
in front of it with a smug smile
like other tourists— "That's it,"
without seeing any of the scenes
described in the lines.

Crows too languid to cry, sweating
under the scorching sun.

---

* Zhang Ji (active c. 750), a Tang dynasty poet, is especially known
for his poem "Mooring by the Maple Bridge at Night."

MEN HAORAN'S SPRING MORNING*

How we have overslept the spring morning!
Here, there, everywhere, birds
are heard twittering.
After a long night's noise
of wind and rain, how many petals
are fallen on the ground?

Pushing aside a tabloid magazine
in a cheap, dubious-looking hotel
in New York, we fold in uneasiness
for a long night punctuated
by latecomers pounding
on the doors, laughing, singing, cursing
along the corridor... and peddlers hawking
their hot dogs in the early morning
with its first gray light revealing
a Chinese actress posing naked in Hollywood
fallen on the floor.

---

* Men Haoran (689-740), a Tang dynasty poet. A poem of his is
entitled "Spring Morning."

DRINK TO LI BAI[*]

You find yourself—more often than not—
drunk, so you believe, at least,
you may invite the moon to dance
with your lonely shadow.

At the high tide of life, let us fill
every minute with joy.
Let not the golden goblet
stand untouched, reflecting
the moon, in vain,
in isolation.

You soar out of yourself
with your poems shining like feathers...

I, too, have tried—drinking,
and dashing a watch against the red wall
of the night-covered Forbidden City
without stopping the time,
or producing a single line. Not like you,
I drown myself in a cup.

---

[*] Li Bai (701-762), a well-known Tang dynasty poet, wrote a large
number of poems about drinking.

THINKING OF LI SHANGYIN AT YADDO[*]

About loss, Li Shangyin is never wrong.
The feelings, confused then and there,
may never be recaptured...
The illusion of the autumn mountains
dissolving in the rain, the moment
of the spring wine warming
against her slender fingers, the regret
about lacking a colorful phoenix's wings,
the fantasy of a camel's shadow trudging, off
and on, across the bronze mirror,
the reading deep into the night,
with the moonlight chill
on her bare arms, the discovery
of one's self helpless drifting
like a tumbleweed, the vision of a pearl
holding tears in the azure ocean,
and of the decorated zither
having half the strings broken, each string,
each peg, reminiscent
of the wasted years...

---

[*] Li Shangyin (812-858), a late Tang dynasty poet, especially known

At Yaddo, Li Shangyin walks out
of the lonely woods into my cabin, where
the world bursts into a candle spark, where
a butterfly wakes out of a dream.

---

for the elusive spatial structure of images in his poetry.

70

READING LI SHANGYIN AT NIGHT

When it rains in the mountains, and
the candle light that remembers
your trimming fingers flicks
by the western window,
and the autumn pool is swollen
with missing thoughts, again,
I hear you asking the same question:
"When can you come back?"

Oh, back home—
to tell you about the moment
when you become the mountain,
and the mountain becomes you, deep
in the night, the candle light illuminating
the autumn pool of thoughts swelling
out the western window, and
the rain patters on, repeating
your question.

71

FANTASIES ABOUT XUE TAO*

The man who marries Xue Tao
marries not a poetess.

Not that she has to rhyme herself
through his hiccups
and to punctuate her day and night
to his meaning, but that
a new line always reminds him
of other lines written, once,
for other men, writhing
against the passionate night—
she dares not to close her eyes
even when she comes
lest his suspicions run wild again...

Even a kiss from her
becomes a kitten
liable to scratch, and to bite
into his imagination.

---

* Xue Tao (?-834?), a Tang dynasty courtesan poet, well-known for
her love poetry.

AFTER SU SHI[*]

When you wonder at the possibility of waking
out of the never-ending cycle of old joy,
new grief, the maple leaves falling
cold into the Wu river, when the lone star
hangs on the sparse tung twigs,
witnessing an apparition
of a solitary wild goose wandering
like a hermit, trying each
of the chilly boughs
without choosing to perch;
when you envision the moment
of someone else, another night, sighing
over the story of your life,
with this same yellow pavilion silhouetted
against the night; when a swallow flies
to the silent window framing
the silk fan in her hand, both white
as jade; when you stand
with the shadow of the locust tree moving
into the afternoon; when you question the moon
waning and waxing with the people
in separation, unaware of the time

---

[*] Su Shi (1037-1101), a Song dynasty poet.

flowing away like water

in the dark, when your wife fails

 to recognize you—with your face dust-covered,

your temples frost white

in a dream of reunion by her graveside—

You sigh, and I echo—

There is no self to claim

amidst all the cares of the world,

the night deep, the wind still, no ripples in the river.

LIU YONG'S RELEVANCE*

Little changed, after so many years,
even the screech of cicadas, still comes
so chill, falling through your fingertips
wet with the unexpected rain.

Cicadas screech in a chill, shrill note,
after a sudden shower. We come to a roadside
pavilion
in the evening, about to part
outside the city gate,
with no mood for the farewell drink,
nor heart to tear ourselves apart,
when a boatman's call from the magnolia boat
urges me to board. We gaze
into each other's eyes
in tears, hand holding hand,
our words choked. I'm sailing out,
sailing for thousands and thousands of miles
along the mist-enveloped waves,
the somber dusk haze
deepening against the boundless southern sky.

---

* Liu Yong (987-1053), a Song dynasty poet.

Déjàvu? We live in a world
of words—conjunctives, dangling
modifiers, or fragments.
Nowhere else is so attractive
as a poetic projection
of our prosaic selves in the lines.

It's always hard for lovers to part
since time immemorial.
How much more so at this cold, deserted autumn!
Tonight, where shall I find
myself, waking from the hangover—
against the riverbank lined with weeping willows
the moon sinking,
and the dawn rising on a breeze?
Year after year, I will be far away from you.
All the beautiful scenes are unfolding,
but to no avail.
Oh, to whom can I speak
of the ineffably enchanting landscape?

To whom can I raise
the inexpressible question
sounding like a cicada
frozen in the winter?

TRANSLATION OF MA ZHIYUAN*

Withered vines, old trees, crows at dusk,
a small bridge over the flowing water, a few houses,
an ancient path, the west wind, a lean horse,
and the sun setting...

A heart-broken traveler at the end of the world.

You have left all these nouns
like building blocks, for me to put them
together, in another language,
in another land, the moon setting...

The end of the world in a heart-hardened traveler.

---

* Ma Zhiyuan (1250-1321), a Yuan dynasty poet.

COMPARATIVE POETICS*

It takes the fall of a city
for Xiao and Shen to fall in love,
and the studies of William Empson
to read Guan Daoshen's lines —then to learn
how to make pottery
of the mixed Oriental and Occidental.

*Out of the same chunk
of clay, shape a you,
shape a me. Crush us
both into clay again, mix
it with water, reshape
a you, reshape a me.
So, I have you in my body,
and you'll have me forever in yours, too.*

---

* Xiao and Shen are two characters in a short story of mine, and I
discovered the Song dynasty poet Guan Daoshen's "You and I" after I
learned about William Empson's high opinion of it. I then translated
Guan's poem into English. It is also a convention of Chinese poetics,
however, to read a love poem not merely as a love poem.

78